Persuasion

Persuasion

"Master the Art of Influence In Any Conversation"

PETER THOMSON

Contents

Contents

Introduction

The truth today:

The ability to persuade effectively is more crucial than ever. Whether you're a business owner, salesperson, manager, or simply someone looking to improve your communication skills, mastering the art of persuasion can open doors and create opportunities you never thought possible.

But what exactly is persuasion?

Is it a natural talent that some people are born with or a skill that can be learned and honed? In this book, we'll explore together how persuasion is both an art and a science - a delicate balance of intuition and technique, of emotional intelligence and strategic thinking.

Persuasion

Drawing from my 50+ years of business experience and numerous interactions with clients, colleagues, and fellow experts, I'll share with you the tried, tested, and proven ideas that have helped me and many others become more persuasive in print, in person, and even on Zoom.

As you start this journey…

I encourage you to have a notebook (or digital version) ready for taking down the ideas that resonate with you. Remember, "Even the bluntest pencil is sharper than the sharpest memory." This isn't just a catchy phrase; it's a fundamental truth about how we learn and retain information. When you write something down, you're not just creating a record – you're engaging with the material in a way that helps cement it in your mind.

Throughout this book, we'll examine the psychology behind effective persuasion, exploring concepts like the contrast principle and the power of questions. You'll learn how to read subtle cues and understand what truly motivates people to make decisions.

We'll also discuss practical methods…

You can start using these methods immediately, from crafting the perfect opening to reading body language. And importantly, we'll tackle the ethical

Introduction

considerations that should guide all our persuasive efforts.

This book isn't about manipulating others or using underhanded tactics to get what you want. Instead, it's about communicating more effectively, understanding the needs and motivations of others, and creating win-win situations that benefit everyone involved.

Whether you're looking to close more sales, lead more effectively, or simply improve your personal relationships, the principles and techniques in this book will give you the tools you need to persuade with confidence, integrity, and success.

So, are you ready to begin this journey to persuasion mastery? Let's get going and unlock the secrets of influential communication together.

FREE Bonus:

The W.H.H.A.M Template: Keeps you on track to any goal you've set

What if you had a proven formula to achieve any goal, just by following a simple 5-step process? Imagine being able to set, work toward, and accomplish your most ambitious goals with clarity and precision.

That's exactly what David Store, my highly successful bank manager shared with me over 35 years ago.

This system was so effective that David credited it as *"the best thing he had learned for achieving any goal in life."*

Now, this same formula has evolved into my **W.H.H.A.M** process.

I've refined this process to include powerful elements of motivation, such as leveraging "toward and away" techniques, helping you stay focused while avoiding pitfalls.

Ready to Create Your Success Story?

Download your copy of the **W.H.H.A.M** template today and unlock a simple yet effective way to achieve your goals, whether personal or professional.

Download it here:

www.peterthomson.com/persuasionbonuses

Or scan the QR code below:

If you're enjoying this book, why not check out Peter Thomson's Book **paid! Reveals:** The 10 Secrets for Being Richly Rewarded for the Value you Deliver and the Cascading Impact You Make in Our World.

Are you tired of not getting paid what you're worth?

Frustrated with clients who undervalue your expertise? Now's the time to unlock the real value of your skills with **paid!** – a powerful roadmap to transform how you're compensated for the impact you make.

With **paid!**, Peter reveals the proven methods that have helped professionals increase their income by over 500%—and become the go-to expert in their field without years of trial and error. Now, it's your turn.

Don't Just Work for Time – Get Paid for the Value You Deliver.

In **paid!**, You'll Discover:

- How to Raise Your Fees Without Losing Clients (see page 71)

- How to Attract a Stream of 'Right Fit' Clients (see page 179)

- The 7 Proven Models for Positioning Yourself and Your Fees

Plus, When You Get **paid!**, You'll Also Receive These FREE Bonuses:

- Access to a Bonus Webinar, "**paid! explained!**" – where Peter walks you through the powerful mindset shifts needed to get richly rewarded for the value you deliver.

- 21 Ways to Increase the Average Order Frequency and 50 Ways to Retain Clients

- The Client Gathering Document – a game-changing tool to help you attract and keep your ideal clients.

If that idea excites and intrigues you, then pop over to: www.thepaidbook.com

Chapter 1

The Power of Presentation and Historical Lessons

The Importance of Presentation

Before we examine the core principles of persuasion, let's talk about the power of presentation. In our increasingly digital world, how we present ourselves, ideas and thoughts can make a significant difference in how our message is received.

Consider, for instance...

The world of video conferencing. A small detail, like adding a touch of flair to how your name appears on screen, can set you apart. It shows attention to detail and subtly communicates that you're not just another 'face in a digital box'.

This ties into a broader point about persuasion: presentation matters. Whether you're in a physical meeting room or connecting through a screen, how you present yourself and your ideas can significantly impact how they're received. It's not about flashy gimmicks; it's about thoughtful, intentional choices that enhance your message. As a result, you will raise your profile, positioning, and credibility in any industry.

A Powerful Lesson from Business History

To illustrate some fundamental principles of persuasion and marketing, let's take a journey through business history. Here's a story that revolves around a man who changed the course of business: Asa Griggs Candler.

In the late 19th century, Candler, a pharmacist, and businessman, crossed paths with another pharmacist named John Pemberton. Pemberton had developed a formula for a coca wine, which he later modified into a non-alcoholic beverage.

The Power of Presentation and Historical Lessons

This beverage would eventually become known as Coca-Cola.

Pemberton, however, saw his creation primarily as a product to be sold. Candler, on the other hand, saw something more. In 1888, Candler made a payment of $238.98 for three things:

1. A large jam kettle
2. A stirring spoon
3. The ingredient list – the formula

The full payment eventually came to $2,300.

Now, you might be thinking, "That doesn't sound like much." But let's put it in perspective. In today's money, that would be about $74,669. When you consider that the Coca-Cola business today is valued at $261 billion, I think we can safely say it was a pretty good investment!

But here's where the story gets really interesting, and where we start to see some powerful lessons about persuasion and marketing.

The Secret Ingredient

What one ingredient did Candler add to Coca-Cola that made it the worldwide phenomenon it is today?

When I ask this question, I get all sorts of answers. Sugar is a common guess. Some people even say cocaine – and they're not entirely wrong, as the original formula did contain a small amount of cocaine, which was later removed. Some suggest bubbles to make the distinct fizz of Coca-Cola.

But the real answer is much simpler and much more powerful. Here it is:

Marketing.

Candler understood that the product itself was only part of the equation. The real magic lay in how that product was presented to the world. He didn't just buy a recipe; he bought an opportunity to tell a story, to create an experience, to build a brand.

The Power of Marketing

This is a crucial lesson for you and me and everyone in business, whether selling a product, a service, or even an idea. The quality of what you're offering is important, of course. But equally important – and sometimes even more so – is how you present it to the world. It's about the story you tell, the emotions you evoke, the connections you create.

Think about it: there are countless cola drinks in the world. Many of them, in blind taste tests, are indistinguishable from Coca-Cola. Some people even prefer the taste of other brands. So why does Coca-Cola continue to dominate the market? It's not about the recipe – it's about the marketing. It's about the brand they've built, the associations they've created and the place they've carved out in popular culture.

This is the power of persuasion at its finest.

It's not about tricking people or manipulating them. It's about creating a narrative so compelling that people want to be part of it. It's about understanding human psychology, then tapping into desires and aspirations; about creating connections that go beyond the simple transaction of buying a product, or even a service.

Persuasion

As we go deeper into the art and science of persuasion in the following chapters, I urge you to keep the lesson of the Coca-Cola story in mind. The way you present your ideas, products or yourself, can be just as important as the substance behind them. Mastering this balance is key to becoming truly persuasive.

CHAPTER 2

The Journey of Continuous Learning

The Importance of Continuous Learning

After 50+ years in business, I've had my share of successes and failures. I've ridden the highs and weathered the lows. And if there's one thing I've learned, it's this:

I don't have all the answers.

That might sound strange coming from someone who specialises in helping people get paid for the value they deliver and the cascading impact they make in our world. But it's the truth, and I think it's an important truth to acknowledge.

No one has all the answers. The world of business, like the world at large, is constantly changing. What worked yesterday might not work today, and what works today might be obsolete tomorrow.

That's why I consider myself, first and foremost, a lifelong learner. And I bet you are the same. That's why you're reading this book – not because I have all the answers, but because we're on this journey of discovery together.

I have some great questions, and I have some good answers. I have experiences to share and insights to offer. Even more than that, I have a passion for learning, for exploring, for constantly seeking new and better ways of doing things. It is my hope that's something that resonates with who are you too.

The Difference Between Success and Struggle

Let's talk about success. Specifically, let's talk about what makes the difference between those who struggle and successful consultants, business owners and entrepreneurs. It's a question I've considered a lot over the years, and I think it's worth exploring together.

What do you think makes the difference?

- Is it the service they offer?
- The level of service?
- Maybe it's about location, age or appearance?
- Could it be gender?
- Some other demographic factor?

These are all valid considerations, and they can all play a role. However, in my experience, the real differentiators often go deeper. They're things such as:

1. Self-belief and mindset: The most successful people I've met have an unshakeable belief in themselves and what they're offering. They see obstacles as challenges to overcome, not roadblocks.

2. Proactivity: They don't wait for opportunities to come to them – they go out and create opportunities.

3. Visibility: In today's crowded marketplace, being good isn't enough. We need to be seen.

The most successful people understand the importance of putting themselves out there.

4. Marketing prowess: This ties back to our Coca-Cola story. It's not just about having a great product or service – it's about knowing how to present it to the world.

5. Knowledge and expertise: Successful people never stop learning. They're always honing their skills, always staying on top of the latest developments in their field.

6. Confidence: This is different from arrogance. It's about having faith in your abilities and the value you bring.

7. Personality: Let's face it – people buy from people they like. The ability to connect with others on a personal level can make a huge difference.

But if I had to boil it down to one key factor, I'd say it's this:

"Their ability to market and sell their products and services effectively"

After all...

Marketing brings a potential client to you, often ready, willing and able to buy what you have to offer. And then the selling part? That's persuasion. That's what we're here to explore together – persuasion in print, in person, and even on Zoom.

The Power of Threes

You might have noticed something about the way I phrased that last bit – "in print, in person, and even on Zoom." This wasn't by accident. It's an example of something called "The Rhythm of 3s" or "The Power of 3".

You see, there's something about groups of three that resonates with the human mind. We find it satisfying, memorable and complete. It's why we have sayings like "life, liberty, and the pursuit of happiness" or "blood, sweat, and tears". It's why storytellers talk about a beginning, middle, and end.

In persuasion and communication, this rule of three can be incredibly powerful. It's great for openings – just like when I say I'm going to share:

"Tried and tested and proven ideas."

It's effective for endings too:

"It's been great to be with you; it's been great to share these ideas; it'd be great to spend more time with you again."

This rhythm of 3s is something people naturally respond to. It's pleasing to the ear and easy for the mind to grasp and remember. As we go through these ideas on persuasion together, take note of how this technique is used. More importantly, think about how you can incorporate it into your own communication.

The Essence of Communication

Before we look at the specifics of persuasion, I want to leave you with one fundamental truth about communication. It's something that, once you truly understand it, will transform how you approach every interaction:

**"All communication is an attempt
to persuade someone else to do
or avoid doing something,
either now or in the future."**

Think about that for a moment.

Whether you're giving a sales pitch, drafting an email, having a conversation with a friend, or even posting on social media – you're always trying to persuade. You're trying to get someone to think, feel and act differently.

When we approach communication with this understan-ding, it changes everything. It makes us more intentional about our words and actions. It makes us think more carefully about our audience and what motivates them. It turns every interaction into an opportunity to practice and refine our persuasion skills.

As we move forward in this book...

Please keep this idea in mind. Whether we're talking about persuasion in print, in person, or even on Zoom, remember that at its core, it's all about influencing thoughts, feelings and actions.

In the next chapter...

We're going to go deeper into specific techniques and strategies for effective persuasion. We'll explore:

- How to shift your mindset about selling
- How to position yourself as an expert in your field, and

- How to use questioning techniques to guide people towards the conclusions you want them to reach.

But for now, let's reflect on what we've covered so far.

- Think about the power of marketing, as illustrated by the Coca-Cola story.
- Consider the qualities that set successful people apart.
- Most importantly, start thinking about every communication as an opportunity to persuade.

Persuasion isn't about manipulation or trickery. It's about understanding human psychology, connecting with people on a deeper level and presenting your ideas in a way that resonates with others. Master these skills, and you'll not only be more successful in business – you'll be more effective in every area of your life.

CHAPTER 3

The Art of Persuasion

From Private Investigator to Persuasion Expert

My Unconventional Journey

My journey in business began in an unusual place - as a private investigator involved in bugging and debugging. This experience, while seemingly unrelated to sales and persuasion, taught me a crucial lesson: the importance of having a compelling opening to any conversation with a potential client.

Let me share a story that illustrates this point.

Persuasion

Years ago, when I was in the car phone business - back when it was still "press to speak, release to listen" - I developed a technique that proved incredibly effective.

I'd wander around without a jacket, sleeves rolled up, carrying a notebook instead of a briefcase. I'd spot men (it was mostly men in those days) getting into high-end cars. Then, slightly out of breath and with an air of excitement, I'd run up to them and say:

"Excuse me! Excuse me!"

They'd turn, curious, and ask, "Yes, can I help you?"

I'd reply, breathlessly, "Yes! Can I use your car phone?"

Inevitably, they'd say, "I haven't got a car phone."

That was my cue. "Come with me," I'd say, and lead them to my car where I'd proceed to demonstrate the phone and sell it to them.

This experience hammered home the importance of catching people's attention right from the start. It's a lesson that's served me well throughout my career, and one I hope you'll take to heart as well.

From Car Phones to Leasing: The Birth of Compass Leasing PLC

My success in the car phone business led me into the world of leasing. In 1984, I started what would become Compass Leasing PLC. We grew rapidly, eventually employing 65 people. Our office? An old garage I'd bought and converted. It wasn't fancy to start with, but it was ours, and it was where we built our success.

Picture this: rows of desks, phones ringing constantly, the buzz of deals being made. We had a good number for our time - you could tell how long ago it was because our phone number started with 021 instead of 0121 as it does today for Birmingham numbers. Those were exciting times, full of growth and possibilities.

After just 5 years of hard work and growth, I sold the business for over £4 million. I was 42 years old, and I thought I was set for life. I was ready to retire and enjoy the fruits of my labour. But life, as it often does, had other plans.

The Setback That Led to a New Beginning

The company I sold Compass Leasing to a main board London-based public company. It seemed like a safe bet. But then, their shares fell from the sky like a free-falling safe. In what felt like the blink of an eye, I lost £3 million of my sale proceeds. Just like that, my dreams of early retirement went up in smoke.

It was a tough pill to swallow. But looking back, I realise it was one of the best things that could have happened to me. Why? Because it forced me to start again, and in doing so, it led me to discover my true passion.

I asked myself a crucial question: "What do I love doing?" The answer was clear – I loved speaking, sharing ideas, and helping others succeed. This realisation led me to create my first program, "Action is the Key," a series of 30 cassettes, which I sold alongside my sales training programs.

Each box contained two cassettes, filled with the knowledge and strategies I'd learned over the years. It might seem outdated now, but back then, it was cutting edge.

From Cassettes to Nightingale-Conant: A New Chapter

My venture into audio programs caught the attention of Nightingale-Conant, the renowned personal development publishing company. While they weren't interested in my sales program, they liked my voice and approach. They asked me to do something that, for me, was akin to being asked to rewrite the Bible - they wanted me to re-voice Earl Nightingale's classic "Lead the Field" for the UK market.

Earl Nightingale is often referred to as the father of personal development. His work has influenced millions, me included. In fact, my encounter with Nightingale's "Lead the Field", in 1985, played a significant role in helping me sell my business five years later.

This opportunity with Nightingale-Conant marked the beginning of my career in sharing ideas on a larger scale. It eventually led to the creation of "The Achiever's Edge," which I believe was the world's first audio newsletter.

The Mindset Shift: From Selling to Allowing People to Buy

Through years of experience and learning from mentors, I've developed a three-part system that I believe is key to effective persuasion. It's a system that <u>completely transforms how you approach sales and client interactions.</u>

Let me explain it for you:

1. Learn how to sell:
This might seem obvious, but it's crucial to understand the process thoroughly. This includes mastering what I call the OGPACF framework (Open, Gather, Present, Adjust, Conclude, Follow), understanding NLP (Neuro-Linguistic Programming), and recognising convincer patterns.

We need to know the mechanics of selling inside and out. It's like learning to play an instrument - you need to know the scales before you can improvise.

2. Stop selling:
Now, this might sound counterintuitive, especially after I just told you to learn how to sell. But hear me out. People don't want to be sold to; they want to buy from people they know, like and trust. The moment someone feels they're being "sold to," defences go up and trust goes down.

It's like when you walk into a store and the salesperson immediately pounces on you - doesn't it make you want to turn around and walk out?

3. Allow people to buy:
This is where the magic happens.

"Treat people as though they have already said yes, not as though they will say yes."

This subtle shift in mindset changes everything about how you interact with potential clients. It's about creating an environment where buying feels like the natural next step, not something you're pushing them towards.

Let me give you an example of how this works in practice.

Imagine you're meeting with a potential client. Instead of going in with a rehearsed sales pitch, you approach the meeting as if they've already decided to work with you.

Your conversation might start like this:

"I'm excited about our project together. Before we dive into the details, I'd love to hear more about your vision and goals. What does success look like for you?"

Do you see how different that feels from a traditional sales approach? You're not trying to convince them to buy; you're already talking about working together. It's a powerful shift.

**"Don't try to convince people.
Be convincing."**

Overview of NLP

NLP, or Neuro-Linguistic Programming, is a psychological approach developed in the 1970s by Dr Richard Bandler and Dr John Grinder. It's based on the idea that there's a connection between neurological processes ('neuro'), language ('linguistic'), and behavioural patterns learned through experience ('programming'). In essence, NLP suggests that these elements can be changed to achieve specific goals in life.

The Art of Persuasion

In the context of persuasion and communication, NLP offers several valuable insights:

1. Rapport building: NLP techniques can help you establish quick connections with others by mirroring their body language, speech patterns, and preferred sensory language (visual, auditory, or kinaesthetic).

2. Language patterns: NLP identifies specific language patterns that can influence how information is perceived and processed by the listener.

3. Reframing: This involves changing the context or meaning of a situation to alter its perceived impact, often leading to new behavioural choices.

4. Anchoring: This technique associates a specific touch, sound or image with a particular emotional state, allowing you to potentially trigger that state in yourself or others.

5. Modelling: NLP encourages studying and replicating the behaviours, mindsets and strategies of successful individuals to achieve similar results.

Persuasion

By incorporating NLP principles into your communication, you can enhance your ability to connect with others, understand their perspectives, and present your ideas in ways that resonate more deeply. However, it's crucial to use these techniques ethically, always aiming for mutually beneficial outcomes rather than manipulation.

In the next chapter, we'll go further into these principles and explore more techniques for mastering the art of persuasion. Remember, the goal isn't to trick or manipulate, but to create genuine connections and mutually beneficial relationships. That's the true essence of effective persuasion.

Chapter 4

Advanced Persuasion Techniques

The Power of "Next" and the Golden Rule of Business

One of my mentors, the late great Ted Nicholas, taught me a powerful four-letter word: "Next". Sometimes, the best thing you can do is recognise when a prospect isn't a good fit and move on. It's not about trying to convince everyone to buy from you; it's about finding the right matches.

This ties into what I call the golden rule of business:

DDWT: "Don't Deal With Tossers."

Now, I know that might sound a bit harsh but hear me out.

Be selective with your clients. While I've sometimes phrased this more colourfully as 'Don't Deal With Tossers,' the essence is this: Focus your energy on clients who value your expertise and are not just looking for the lowest price. Life's too short, and your time is too valuable to invest it in relationships where your value isn't appreciated.

This approach allows you to serve your best clients more effectively and build more rewarding business relationships. I'm certainly not advocating this strategy for everyone.

Transactional Customers vs. Relational Clients

Now, let me introduce you to a concept that transformed my understanding of business relationships. I learned this from Roy H. Williams, known as the "Wizard of Ads". Roy (one of the true marketing geniuses) taught me the crucial difference between transactional customers and relational clients.

Transactional customers...

Consider themselves experts and buy primarily on price. They view each interaction as a one-time deal, often playing suppliers against each other to get the lowest possible price. They don't care if the supplier makes a profit or stays in business long-term. It's all about the deal for them.

Relational clients...

Look to you as the expert. They consider price as a factor, but not the factor. They value long-term relationships and are often willing to pay more for quality, reliability, and expertise. These are the clients who will stick with you through thick and thin, who see you as a partner in their success.

Let me give you an example to illustrate this difference.

Imagine you're selling a car.

A transactional customer might come in with printouts of the lowest prices they've found online, demanding you match or beat them. They're not interested in your expertise or the value-added services you might offer. It's all about the numbers for them.

A relational client, however, might come in saying, "I've heard great things about your dealership. I'm looking for a car that will be reliable for my family, and I trust your expertise to guide me to the right choice." You can see the difference? This client is looking for a relationship, not just a transaction.

Our goal should be to position ourselves in the market to attract these relational clients. This doesn't mean never engaging in transactional sales, but rather focusing our energy and marketing efforts on cultivating relationships with clients who value what we bring to the table beyond just the product or service itself.

The Art of Questioning: Your Secret Weapon in Persuasion

Now, let's talk about one of the most powerful tools in your persuasion toolkit: the art of asking well-crafted questions.

Many people think selling is all about talking and presenting your product or service. But the most effective selling happens when you're listening, not talking.

The selling process actually takes place in the gathering stage, not the presenting stage.

"Allow people to convince themselves through their answers to your well-crafted questions."

It's like the old saying goes, "No one likes to be sold, but everyone likes to buy."

Here's a powerful insight about questioning that I want you to remember:

"When you make a statement followed by a question, if somebody answers the question, they don't question the statement."

Let me give you an example:

Statement: "People tell me I am the most prolific business development author in the UK."

Question: "Have you seen my website about my latest book?"

If the person answers the question (whether yes or no), they implicitly accept the preceding statement. They're not questioning whether you're really the most prolific business development author; they're just focusing on whether they've seen your website.

This technique can be incredibly powerful when used ethically to establish credibility or frame a conversation. But remember, with great power comes great responsibility. Use this technique to highlight genuine strengths and establish real credibility, not to mislead.

Positioning Yourself as an Expert: The Three Key Elements

In today's crowded marketplace, being seen as an expert in your field is more important than ever. But how do you establish yourself as an expert?

Here are 3 key elements:

1. Walk like an expert:
This is about how you carry yourself. Confidence is key, but it's not about arrogance. It's about having a quiet assurance that comes from knowing your stuff. Stand tall, make eye contact, and move with purpose.

2. Talk like an expert:
This doesn't mean using jargon to confuse people. On the contrary, true experts can explain complex concepts simply. Use industry terminology appropriately, but always be ready to explain things in layperson's terms. Remember, the goal is to communicate, not to impress.

3. Write a book:
This might seem daunting, but it's one of the most powerful ways to establish your credibility. All recognised experts have books. It doesn't have to be a 500-page tome; even a short, focused book on your area of expertise can make a huge difference.

A book is like a business card on steroids - it opens doors and establishes your authority like nothing else.

Let me share a personal anecdote about the power of having a book.

Years ago, I was on a plane journey back from Los Angeles and was seated next to the sales and advertising director for a major newspaper. We got to chatting and had a great conversation throughout the flight. When I got back, I sent him a signed copy of my latest book. As you would expect, I followed up and he engaged me to speak for his senior management team. That session went well and he asked me to fly to Sweden to keynote their yearly sales conference.

I also have many other stories as well about the Power that's created by being an author. After all, the first six letters of the word authority are -Author!

Your marketing efforts should be focused on bringing the right people into the top of your funnel - people who are ready, willing and able to buy because of how you've positioned yourself in the market. And nothing positions you better than being seen as a published expert in your field.

In the next chapter...

We'll explore more advanced persuasion techniques, including how to use the power of storytelling and emotional connection to enhance your persuasive abilities. Remember, mastering these skills is a journey, not a destination. Keep practicing, keep refining, and most importantly, keep learning.

CHAPTER 5

Advanced Persuasion Techniques

The Art of Communication

The Power of Relational Thinking: The Labyrinth Approach

Let's explore a concept that can transform how you think about your communication process. Think of your communication process as a monocursal labyrinth rather than a multicursal maze.

What's the difference?

A labyrinth has one path that leads from the outside to the centre or the other side. You might encounter twists and turns, but there's only one path. A maze, on the other hand, has multiple paths and dead ends.

This labyrinth approach aligns perfectly with the OGPACF (Open, Gather, Present, Adjust, Conclude, Follow) sales process. It's about guiding your client through a journey, not leaving them confused or lost or unwilling to make a decision.

Here's how this plays out in practice:

1. Open: This is where you set the stage for the conversation. It's like the entrance to the labyrinth.

2. Gather: Here, you're asking questions, learning about your client's needs, wants and concerns. You're guiding them along the path.

3. Present: Now you're showing how your product or service meets their needs. You're moving towards the centre of the labyrinth.

4. Adjust: This is where you address any worries or objections. You're navigating the twists and turns.

5. Conclude: You're reaching an agreement. You're nearing the centre of the labyrinth.

6. Follow: This is your follow-up, ensuring client satisfaction. You've reached the centre and are maintaining the relationship.

By thinking of your sales process as a labyrinth, you ensure that every step leads naturally to the next. There are no dead ends, no confusing choices. You're guiding your client on a journey of discovery that leads to a natural conclusion - working with you.

Practical Application: The Power of Assumption

To put these principles into practice, I want you to try something the next time you walk into a meeting with a new client.

Imagine this scenario:

Before you even start the conversation...

The client says, "I've researched you, spoken to your other clients, and looked into your offerings. I just want to say, I'm going to buy what you have. You'd have to really upset me for me not to buy."

How different would your approach be in this situation?

You'd probably feel more relaxed and confident. You'd focus on understanding their needs and how you can best serve them, rather than trying to convince them to buy.

This is exactly how I approach every client interaction - as if they've already decided to buy. It changes everything about the conversation. It's not about being presumptuous; it's about being confident in the value we offer and focusing on how we can best serve the client.

The Contrast Principle

Let's talk about a powerful persuasion technique called the contrast principle. I learned about this years ago and later discussed it with Professor Robert Cialdini, a renowned expert in the field of influence and persuasion.

The contrast principle states:

"It's what you say before you say what you mean to say that makes the difference."

But it goes beyond just words. It's also what you do before you do what you mean to do that makes the difference. In essence, it's about creating the right climate for ethical persuasion to take place.

When I interviewed Bob Cialdini for my Achiever's Edge program, I noticed he frequently used the words "before" and "then." This is the essence of the contrast principle in action. You set up a context "before" that makes what comes "then" more impactful.

This principle is particularly important when discussing money.

"Without contrast, everything can sound either expensive or cheap"

Persuasion

We need to take control of the financial thinking of the other person by providing context.

We can create contrast by discussing:

- Outcomes: What will happen if they implement your solution versus if they don't?

- Potential downsides: What are the risks of not taking action?

- Other ways of getting results: How does your solution compare to alternatives? Value of time: How much time will your solution save them?

- Effort required: How much easier will their life/work be with your solution?

- Impact on reputation: How will your solution enhance their standing in their industry?

By setting up the right contrast, we can help our clients better understand and appreciate the value of what we're offering.

For instance, if you're selling a high-end consulting package, you might contrast it with the cost of making a bad decision or the opportunity cost of not improving their business processes.

The Art of Closing

Many people struggle with closing, often due to fear of rejection, lack of confidence or fear of success. But remember, if you've been treating the person as if they've already said yes throughout the conversation, closing becomes much easier.

Here are a couple of gentle closing techniques:

1. "When might you like to start?"
2. "Is that something you might be open to?"

These questions are non-threatening and allow the client to visualise moving forward with you. They're not pushy, but they do move the conversation towards a decision.

Remember, we're <u>not</u> trying to convince anyone or force a decision. That's not ethical selling; it's manipulation. As the saying goes,

"A person convinced against their will is of the same opinion still."

Instead, our goal should be to create an environment where saying "yes" feels like the natural next step.

This is why the gathering stage is so crucial. By the time you get to closing, the client should already be largely convinced based on how well you understand their needs and how clearly, you've demonstrated your ability to meet those needs.

In the next chapter...

We'll explore a powerful formula for crafting persuasive written communication: the W.I.S.C.D.A.R. process. This technique can revolutionise how you approach emails, webpages, articles, and various other forms of written persuasion.

You'll learn how to connect with your audience on their wavelength, pique their interest, sell benefits effectively, build conviction through social proof, increase desire, guide readers to take action, and reinforce results.

We'll also examine the concept of 'prestivoxitation' – a unique approach to language that can significantly enhance your persuasive writing.

If you like these ideas in The Persuasion Book, why not check out:

The Persuasion Formula Course
"The Psychology of Influence to Master Any Conversation"

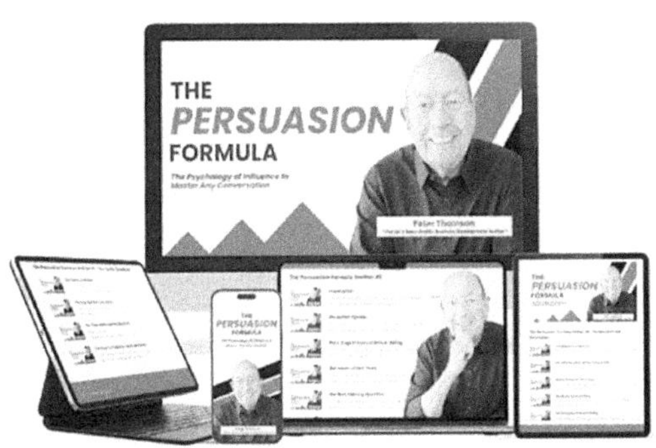

The step-by-step system I used to build and sell my company for enough to retire at 42.

And the same methods my clients have asked me to teach them over the last 30 years so they too can enjoy businesses and lives of choice.

Now you can use these...

Ethically based ideas, methods, templates, and guidance to be authentically and powerfully yourself – in print, in person and even online. **It's just so pleasing when others naturally connect with your ideas and confidently choose your products and services.**

Click here:
https://www.peterthomson.com/the-persuasion-formula

CHAPTER 6

Advanced Persuasion Techniques

The Art of Written Communication

Gary Halbert, the legendary copywriter and direct marketing guru, once said:

**"You're Only One Letter Away
From Striking It Rich."**

With today's digital communication, we might update this to say we're only one email, webpage, webinar, masterclass, Facebook post, or LinkedIn article away. The essence remains the same – we're only one communication away from potential clients and striking gold.

Let me share a personal story that vividly illustrates this point.

Back in 1998, I wrote an eight-page letter using a formula I'm about to share with you. This wasn't some closely guarded secret – I learned it from a free booklet distributed by the British Post Office, of all places! The results? They were, quite frankly, staggering.

The letter promoted my new audio newsletter, "The Achievers Edge". Over the next 13 years, I averaged 1,500 subscribers every month. At £9.97 plus £2.97 VAT per subscription, the math is eye-opening:

13 years x 1,500 subscribers x £13 per month = £3,042,000

That's an average of just under £20,000 a month. Now you can see why I'm a true believer in Gary Halbert's quote!

So, what's this magical formula?

It's called W.I.S.C.D.A.R. Let's break it down:

W – Wavelength

We need to be on the same wavelength as the person who receives our message.

It's about creating a mental environment where they're primed to understand, believe and act on our ideas.

One effective technique is using a pre-head that labels who they <u>are</u>.

For instance:

"Attention Fellow Pet Iguana Lover"

If you're particularly fond of your pet iguana, you'd be hard-pressed not to read every word that follows, wouldn't you?

We can also use the headline to label our audience:

"Why Some Consultants Are Earning £250,000 a
Year
Whilst Others Struggle to Get By"

I – Interest

Next, we need to pique the reader's interest. Focus on the features of your product or service that make it unique or valuable.

S – Sell Benefits

Don't just list features – we explain how the reader will benefit from buying and using our product or service. Paint a vivid picture of the transformation they'll experience. How will their life be different – and better – after using what you're offering?

C – Conviction

People are often persuaded by 'Social Proof'. This is where we add testimonials, case studies, or endorsements from previous purchasers or well-known figures in our field.

Don't underestimate the power of testimonials! When I used to run more seminars than webinars, my promotional webpages would feature between 25 and 100 testimonials from previous attendees. These real-life success stories can be incredibly persuasive.

D – Desire

Now it's time to increase the desire. We need to increase the likelihood of the reader wanting to buy what we're offering. This could involve adding bonuses, special terms, payment plans, or anything else that increases the perceived (and real) value of our offering.

A – Action

We must clearly explain what the reader needs to do to order our product or service. This is where a peculiar word comes into play: prestivoxitation. You might be familiar with prestidigitation, meaning sleight of hand. Well, I coined the term prestivoxitation to mean "sleight of voice".

Now, I know that sounds a bit manipulative, so I've refined it to **"integrity-based prestivoxitation".**

Here's how it works:

You've likely seen order forms that say something like, "Yes, please rush me my copy of product X at the special price of only XX." Notice how the language shifts from addressing you to speaking as you? That's prestivoxitation in action.

By crafting the words in the first person, you encourage the reader to process them as if they wrote them themselves. It's not about trickery – it's about using language elegantly and with integrity (and persuasively) to help people see possibilities they might have missed.

For example, instead of saying "This will cost you X amount," you might say "Your investment in this solution is X amount." The word 'investment' implies future returns, whereas 'cost' implies loss. Both are truthful, but they frame the information differently.

Another example is the use of presuppositions. When you say, "When we start working together" instead of "If we start working together", you're presupposing the collaboration. This can subtly influence the client's thinking without being manipulative.

So, whenever you wish to (with integrity) have the reader process the words as though they wrote them, simply write in the first person, making the reader the author of those words. I am excited to use this technique in my marketing!

(Did you notice how I phrased that sentence?)

R – Results

Finally, we reiterate what the reader is going to get, focusing specifically on the experience, the transformation, and the benefits. A smooth way to present benefits is to precede them with phrases like "now you can…" or "now you can enjoy…". This flows more naturally than the older "which means that…" approach.

And there you have it – the W.I.S.C.D.A.R. process, a proven formula for writing engaging, magnetic and highly-converting copy.

The beauty of this formula is its versatility. You can apply it to nearly any form of communication: emails, webpages, articles, direct mail, videos, webinar scripts, proposals... the list goes on. I'm certain you can think of many more applications in your own business.

Remember, you're only one well-crafted communication away from striking rich. So why not give W.I.S.C.D.A.R. a try? Your next big success might be just one letter, email or webpage away!

In the next chapter...

We'll explore even more advanced techniques, including how to read and use body language effectively in your persuasive communications. Remember, these skills take practice to master. Keep applying these principles, and you'll see your persuasive abilities grow over time.

CHAPTER 7

Advanced Persuasion Techniques

Non-Verbal Cues and Language Mastery

Our previous chapter examined the art of communication, covering the labyrinth approach to steering conversations and the influential role of assumptions. Building on these foundations, we'll now explore advanced techniques that emphasise non-verbal cues and language mastery.

These skills will enhance the strategies we've already discussed, equipping you with a comprehensive toolkit for persuasive communication.

The Lacrimal Caruncle: A Secret Weapon in Face-to-Face Persuasion

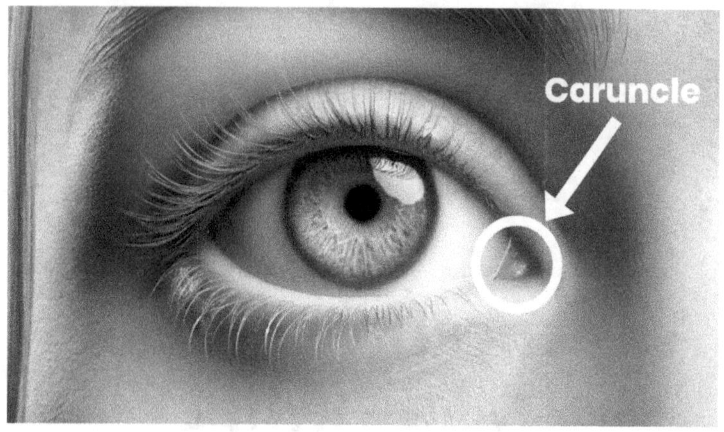

Let me share a little-known secret that can be incredibly powerful in face-to-face interactions. It's called the lacrimal caruncle.

The lacrimal caruncle is that little red bit in the corner of your eye, near your nose. When someone is showing concern, disagreement, or discomfort, this caruncle often disappears as the lower eyelid moves towards the nose and upwards.

This movement is usually subconscious - the person doing it isn't aware they're doing it. But if you're observant, you can spot it. This gives you valuable information about how the other person is feeling.

Here's the golden rule:

"Never ask for a 'yes' unless you can see the caruncle."

If you see the caruncle disappearing, it's a sign that the person may have reservations. In this case, you might want to address their concerns before moving forward.

If you notice this happening, don't point it out directly. That would only make the person self-conscious and potentially defensive. Instead, you might say something like, "Normally, when I'm speaking to somebody about this, they sometimes have questions they want to ask. Is there anything you'd like to clarify?"

This approach acknowledges the unspoken concern without making the person feel exposed. It gives them an opportunity to voice any reservations they might have, allowing you to address these concerns and potentially turn a "no" into a "yes".

Verisimilitude: Truth, Proof and Evidence

Verisimilitude (the appearance of truth) is about providing truth, proof, and evidence. It's crucial in building trust and credibility.

Verisimilitude should be considered whenever we are quoting numbers in our marketing messages. A statement such as: "100s have tried our new miracle system" leaves any readers with a feeling of scepticism.

However: "In a recent study, 965 people scored their satisfaction with our new XXX at over 90%" is more believable.

A Powerful Closing Question:

"Well, let me just ask you. Based on everything we've talked about so far, how do you feel about going ahead?"

This question is powerful because:

1. It references the entire conversation, not just the last few minutes. This reminds the client of all the value you've discussed.

2. It asks about feelings, which often drive decisions more than logic. People make decisions emotionally and justify them logically.

3. It's open-ended, allowing the client to express any lingering concerns. This gives you one last opportunity to address any issues before finalising the deal.

The Importance of Writing a Book

One powerful way to establish yourself as an expert is to write a book. A book serves as a tangible representation of your knowledge and expertise. It's like a business card on steroids - it opens doors and establishes your authority like nothing else.

I've authored several books, including *Sell Your Way to the Top* and *The Secrets of Communication*. These books not only share my ideas but also serve as powerful marketing tools. They give potential clients a deeper understanding of my approach and demonstrate my expertise in a way that a brochure or website simply can't match.

Writing a book doesn't have to be a daunting task. It could be a short, focused book on your area of expertise. The key is to provide value and showcase your unique insights and approaches.

The Golden Goose of Success

Let's conclude with a concept I call "The Golden Goose of Success." This is based on the old fable of the goose that laid golden eggs. The farmer, in his greed, killed the goose to get all the eggs at once, only to find there were no eggs inside. He lost his source of wealth by not understanding where it truly came from.

In business, the 'golden goose' refers to the ideas and processes that produce results. I break this down into what I call:

The WWHAM system:

1. WHAT: What do you want to achieve? Where do you want to end up? These need to be clear, specific and meaningful to you.

2. WHY: What are the motivations, both away and towards, that will drive you to take action towards this goal?

3. HOW: How are you going to achieve this goal? Who needs to be involved? What specific actions do we need to take? These are the day-to-day tasks that, when done consistently, lead to the achievement of our goals. And what systems do we need to put in place to achieve these goals? This might include marketing processes, sales processes, delivery processes, etc.

4. ACTIONS: Now you know what to do, action needs to be taken at the time and date specified in your HOW section.

5. MEASURE: Once action has been taken, measure to make sure you are on track

towards the accomplishment of your goal. There are two distinct types of measurement: Internal (how you feel about your results) and External (the results you can measure, the numbers, the dates, the cash).

By clearly defining your goals, establishing effective processes, and taking consistent steps, you create your own 'golden goose' that will continue to produce results over time.

For example…

Let's say your goal is to double your client base in the next year. Your processes might include a new marketing strategy, a refined sales approach, and an improved client onboarding system. Your steps might include daily social media engagement, weekly blog posts and monthly webinars.

The key is to nurture your 'golden goose' - continually refine your processes, stay committed to your daily steps, and keep your eyes on your goals. Don't be like the farmer who killed the goose for short-term gain. Instead, focus on creating sustainable, long-term success.

In the final section...

We'll tie all these concepts together and provide you with a roadmap for implementing these persuasion techniques in your own business and life.

Remember, mastering persuasion is a journey, not a destination. Keep practicing, keep refining and, most importantly, keep learning.

Your Journey to Persuasion Mastery

As we reach the end of our exploration into the art and science of persuasion, it's time to reflect on the key lessons we've covered and consider how you can apply them in your own life and business.

The Power of Persuasion: A Recap

Throughout this book, we've looked at various aspects of persuasion:

Persuasion

1. We started by understanding that persuasion is both an art and a science, requiring a balance of intuition and technique.

2. We explored the power of marketing, as illustrated by the Coca-Cola story, showing how presentation can be just as important as the product itself.

3. We discussed the importance of continuous learning and the qualities that set successful people apart in the business world.

4. We examined the crucial shift from selling to allowing people to buy, and the power of treating clients as if they've already said yes.

5. We examined advanced techniques like the contrast principle, the art of questioning, and the power of body language cues like the lacrimal caruncle.

6. We explored concepts like verisimilitude and prestivoxitation, showing how to use language effectively and ethically in persuasion.

7. Finally, we discussed the importance of setting clear goals and taking consistent action through the WWHAM system.

Putting It All Together: Your Persuasion Toolkit

Now that you have these tools at your disposal, how do you put them into practice? Here are some steps to help you on your journey to persuasion mastery:

1. Practice Active Listening: Remember, persuasion isn't just about talking. It's about understanding your audience's needs and desires. Let's make a conscious effort to listen more than we speak. Years ago, I used a chess clock to measure how often I was speaking compared to how much my potential client was speaking. I was shocked and learned a valuable lesson!

2. Refine Your Questioning Technique: Start incorporating well-crafted questions into your conversations. Remember, "When you make a statement followed by a question, if somebody answers the question, they don't question the statement."

3. Shift Your Mindset: Start approaching your interactions as if the other person has already decided to work with you. Notice how this changes your behaviour and the overall dynamic.

4. Use the Contrast Principle: Before presenting your ideas or offers, set the stage by providing context that makes your proposition more appealing.

5. Pay Attention to Non-Verbal Cues: In your next face-to-face meeting, practice observing the lacrimal caruncle. Use this information to gauge when to press forward and when to address concerns.

6. Craft Your Language Carefully: Start replacing words like 'cost' with 'investment' and notice how this subtle shift affects your conversations.

7. Set Clear Goals: Use the WWHAM system to set clear, actionable goals for yourself. Remember, it's not just about what you want to achieve, but why you want to achieve it and how you're going to get there.

The Ethical Dimension of Persuasion

As you embark on this journey to enhance your persuasion skills, always remember the ethical dimension of what we've discussed. Persuasion, when used ethically, is about creating win-win situations. It's about helping people make decisions that are genuinely in their best interest.

I'm certain you would never use these techniques to mislead or manipulate. Instead, you'll use them to communicate more effectively, to better understand the needs and motivations of others, and to create mutually beneficial outcomes.

Your Ongoing Journey

Remember, mastering the art of persuasion is not a destination, but a journey. It requires constant practice, refinement, and learning. Like any skill, persuasion improves with time and practice.

Consider keeping a journal of your experiences as you apply these techniques. Note what works well and what doesn't. Reflect on why certain approaches were more effective than others. This self-reflection will be invaluable in your growth process.

A Final Word

As we finish this part of our journey together here, I want to leave you with one final thought. The skills and techniques we've discussed in this book are powerful. They have the potential to significantly impact your personal and professional life. But remember, with great power comes great responsibility.

Use these skills to create positive change, help others and make a meaningful difference in the world. That, ultimately, is the true measure of success in persuasion and in life.

Thank you for joining me on this journey. I'm excited to see how you'll use these skills to enhance your own life and the lives of those around you. Remember, the journey to persuasion mastery is ongoing. Keep learning, keep growing, and keep persuading - ethically and effectively.

I wish you every success in all your adventures in life and to you being rightfully rewarded for the value you deliver and the cascading impact you make in our world.

Peter Thomson Bio

Peter Thomson is regarded as The UK's Leading Strategist on Business and Personal Growth and The UK's Most Prolific Information Product Creator.

Starting in business in 1972 he built 3 successful companies – selling the last to a public company, after only 5 years trading, for £4.2M enabling him to retire at age 42.

Since that time Peter has concentrated on sharing his proven methods for business and personal success via online video programmes, books, seminars, conference speeches and mentoring programmes.

Persuasion

With over 100 audio and 100 video programmes written and recorded he is Nightingale Conant's leading UK author.

In 1999 The American Intercontinental University in London – with permission granted by the American Government- awarded Peter an Honorary Doctorate (Doctor of Letters) for his work in communication skills and helping others to succeed in life. And in 2017 Peter was also awarded a lifetime achievement award by the ISM (Institute of Sales Management)

Peter specialises in helping coaches, consultants, speakers, trainers and small-business owners share more of their authentic messages with more people than they could ever reach on a 1-to-1 basis by showing them how to write and create and market their own informational products and charge the right fee rates.

To talk to Peter, send an email his Marketing Manager Rachel Groves: rachel@peterthomson.com or call +44 (0) 7910 582539

Here's a link to Peter's YouTube channel, so you can see Peter's engaging style: https://www.youtube.com/@PeterThomson/videos

Testimonials

And here are just a few testimonials from previous clients Peter has worked with:

I was a member of Peter's membership programme and also had monthly 1 to 1 sessions at Peter's home (highly recommended!)

Soon into the programme Peter helped me to focus on producing an online video-based product as my strength is presenting and training.

To cut a long story short, through Peter's invaluable, informal and fun mentoring I now have a video programme, the Limbic Performance System (LPS), which has changed my life. I no longer need to train unless I want to, and LPS made around £250,000 in just 1 year from its launch.

Persuasion

Estimated blended sales in the 12 months following were over £1,000,000.

- Steve Neale - BCS International Ltd

"Working with Peter over a period of 18 months I created additional profits of over £100,000 using his ideas."

- Mark Wickersham, Accountant

Pay very close attention to what Peter has to say.
One of his insights alone has had a profound effect on my business:
Turnover before I met Peter: £79,672
Then one year later £267,172
And in the second year £384,442
and that's from just implementing ONE of Peter's suggestions.
If you feel that you are not being rewarded sufficiently for your efforts then you must read PAID! "

- Sylvia Snowling - SDLT Claims Ltd

FREE Bonus:

The W.H.H.A.M Template: Keeps you on track to any goal you've set

What if you had a proven formula to achieve any goal, just by following a simple 5-step process? Imagine being able to set, work toward, and accomplish your most ambitious goals with clarity and precision.

That's exactly what David Store, my highly successful bank manager shared with me over 35 years ago.

This system was so effective that David credited it as *"the best thing he had learned for achieving any goal in life."*

Now, this same formula has evolved into my **W.H.H.A.M** process.

I've refined this process to include powerful elements of motivation, such as leveraging "toward and away" techniques, helping you stay focused while avoiding pitfalls.

Ready to Create Your Success Story?

Download your copy of the **W.H.H.A.M** template today and unlock a simple yet effective way to achieve your goals, whether personal or professional.

Download it here:

www.peterthomson.com/persuasionbonuses

Or scan the QR code below:

If you're enjoying this book, why not check out Peter Thomson's Book ***paid!* Reveals:** The 10 Secrets for Being Richly Rewarded for the Value you Deliver and the Cascading Impact You Make in Our World.

Are you tired of not getting paid what you're worth?

Frustrated with clients who undervalue your expertise? Now's the time to unlock the real value of your skills with ***paid!*** – a powerful roadmap to transform how you're compensated for the impact you make.

With ***paid!***, Peter reveals the proven methods that have helped professionals increase their income by over 500%—and become the go-to expert in their field without years of trial and error. Now, it's your turn.

Don't Just Work for Time – Get Paid for the Value You Deliver.

In ***paid!***, You'll Discover:

- How to Raise Your Fees Without Losing Clients (see page 71)

- How to Attract a Stream of 'Right Fit' Clients (see page 179)

- The 7 Proven Models for Positioning Yourself and Your Fees

Plus, When You Get ***paid!***, You'll Also Receive These FREE Bonuses:

- Access to a Bonus Webinar, "***paid!* explained!**" – where Peter walks you through the powerful mindset shifts needed to get richly rewarded for the value you deliver.

- 21 Ways to Increase the Average Order Frequency and 50 Ways to Retain Clients

- The Client Gathering Document – a game-changing tool to help you attract and keep your ideal clients.

If that idea excites and intrigues you, then pop over to: www.thepaidbook.com

If you like these ideas in The Persuasion Book, why not check out:

The Persuasion Formula Course
"The Psychology of Influence to Master Any Conversation"

The step-by-step system I used to build and sell my company for enough to retire at 42.

And the same methods my clients have asked me to teach them over the last 30 years so they too can enjoy businesses and lives of choice.

Now you can use these...

Ethically based ideas, methods, templates, and guidance to be authentically and powerfully yourself - in print, in person and even online. **It's just so pleasing when others naturally connect with your ideas and confidently choose your products and services.**

Click here:
https://www.peterthomson.com/the-persuasion-formula